The Girl Who Wasn't and Is

THE GIRL WHO WASN'T AND IS

Anastasia Walker

The Girl Who Wasn't and Is

Published by bd-studios.com in New York City, 2022
Copyright © 2022 by Anastasia Walker

Photographs and *Nereid* drawing (p. 18) by Anastasia Walker
Synapse (a Self-Portrait) drawing (p. 72) by Bill Walker
Design by luke kurtis

ISBN 978-1-950231-94-2

All Rights Reserved. No part of this publication may be reproduced, stored in a retrieval system or transmitted in any form or by any means without the prior permission in writing of copyright holders and of the publisher.

Contents

The Girl Who Wasn't and Is	9
Seminality	10
November's Child	13
Medusa	14
"You Have Two Sons"	16
The Girl with Eyes of the Sea	17
To All the Beautyfull Weeds That Won't Grow Straight	20
Love Song (Aversion)	22
AJ's Arms	24
Before You Fall	26
Love Song (Separation 1)	28
Daughter Late (Pietas)	32
Betty Grable Legs	36
Love Song (Dad)	37
Love Song (Separation 2)	38
Love Song (Congruence)	39
The Length of an Arm	41
Hope's the Drug You	42

The Girl Who Vanished in Her Tomorrows	45
Cassandra	47
#WalkingWhile	48
For Muhlaysia	49
Remembrance (January 2013)	51
The Girl Who Dreamed of Tornadoes	54
Night Songs	56
Love Song (Death)	70
i, scattered	71
The Girl Who Collected Feathers	74
Philomela	77
What Is a Wall?	78
9:29 Is Long Enough	80
Lily Law n the Street Queens	81
The Hole	85
Maenad	86
Indivisible	92
The Girl Who Loves Marilyn Monroe	94
The Girls Who Saw the Dinosaur Bones	96
Dancing with Nicky	100
Love Song (Mom)	102
Love Song ( )	104
After and Before (Four Photos) [essay]	109

Notes on the Poems	130
Acknowledgements	133
About the Author	135

The Girl Who Wasn't and Is

She'll smile when you ask why she's crying
And cry when you ask why she smiles
And tell you about a girl
Who lived in a box at the back of a basement
Shelf with her untold years
Hacking her to splinters with axes
'Til the fissures emerged in her face
And she lost the will to die with stoic grace
And snatched the charred pieces
From the furnace flames
A Pygmalion in bricolage
Fashioning with paint and glue
The face glimpsed through the interstices
Between quotidian and fantasy
A fugitive cursing her truth-crossed mirror
And hoarding every stranger's
Polished pleasantries and indifferent glance—
How the sheen of the centuries enhances
The pronoun *she!*—a girl
Waking to a dream of herself

Seminality

so much comes
from that newborn stub
sprays its seed on
the million tongues
say you will be
he you will be
silent you will be
blue

November's Child

The questions flutter
out of the pale blue
air like browned leaves:
child, when did you
feel the chasm yawn
the world recede
when did that voice
start whispering
it's wrong
you're wrong
when did you first
tally your innocence
in the precious minutes
of midges' frolics
in the shivering sun
of an autumn twilight?

Medusa

splintered on a temple rock
by riptides of lust that couldn't care less
and your marble eyed goddess
strewed you in the dirt—girl
now thing, your gold dreads masking
the dark holes where the terror
was seeded, in your charnel heart
one wish: that the cut, when it comes,
wastes his husbandry and leaves you
Whole

"You Have Two Sons"
For Kelly and Kyle

those blue pink white stripes strange &
the words at first opaque—*You have
two sons*—but the quiet, frightened
plea in that look you'd seen
so often, the brows' arch this
time a veil was rent gifting his
crazy, harrowing, magical
Yes

The Girl with Eyes of the Sea

Her eyes were not the blue of the sky or
Brown of the earth but the furtive gray-
Blue-green of the sea, like
The light off its ripples never fixed
But skipping from one to the next
To the next and back and this girl
With eyes of the sea couldn't see
Herself in the usual places—
Mirrors or windows, TV or the faces
Of people she passed who troubled to
Look at her and laugh
Or sneer—or hear herself in the words
She or others spoke or sang. The girl with
The sea's eyes saw her face only
In the shimmering moon on the slumbering bay,
Felt herself in those hushed stoic depths
Drifting past our shores on their way
From wish to wish.

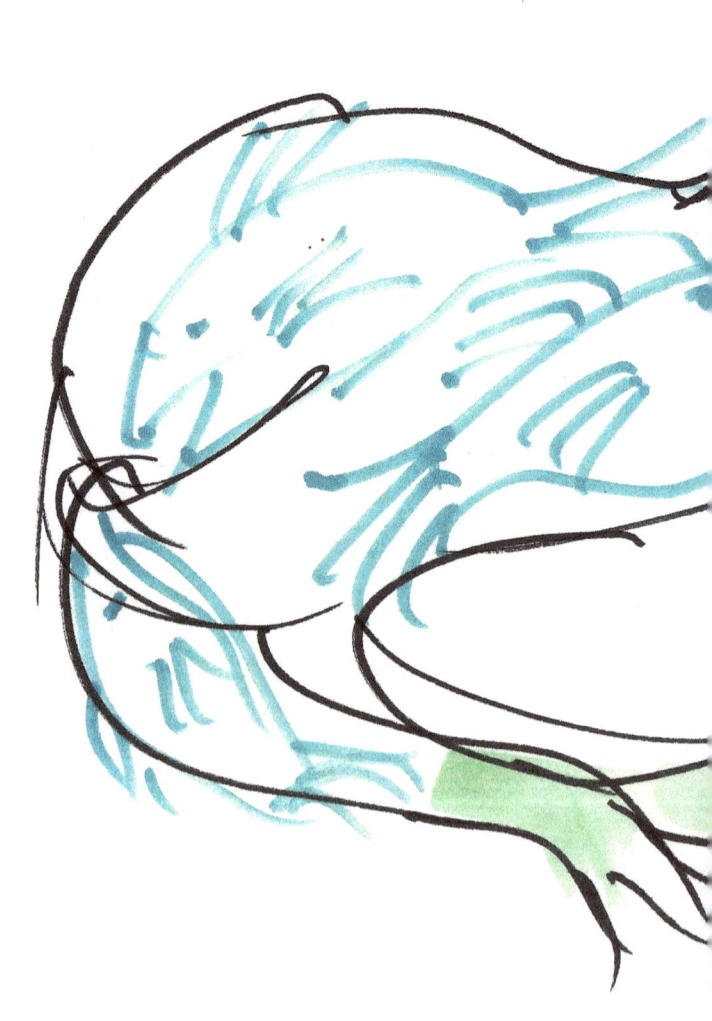

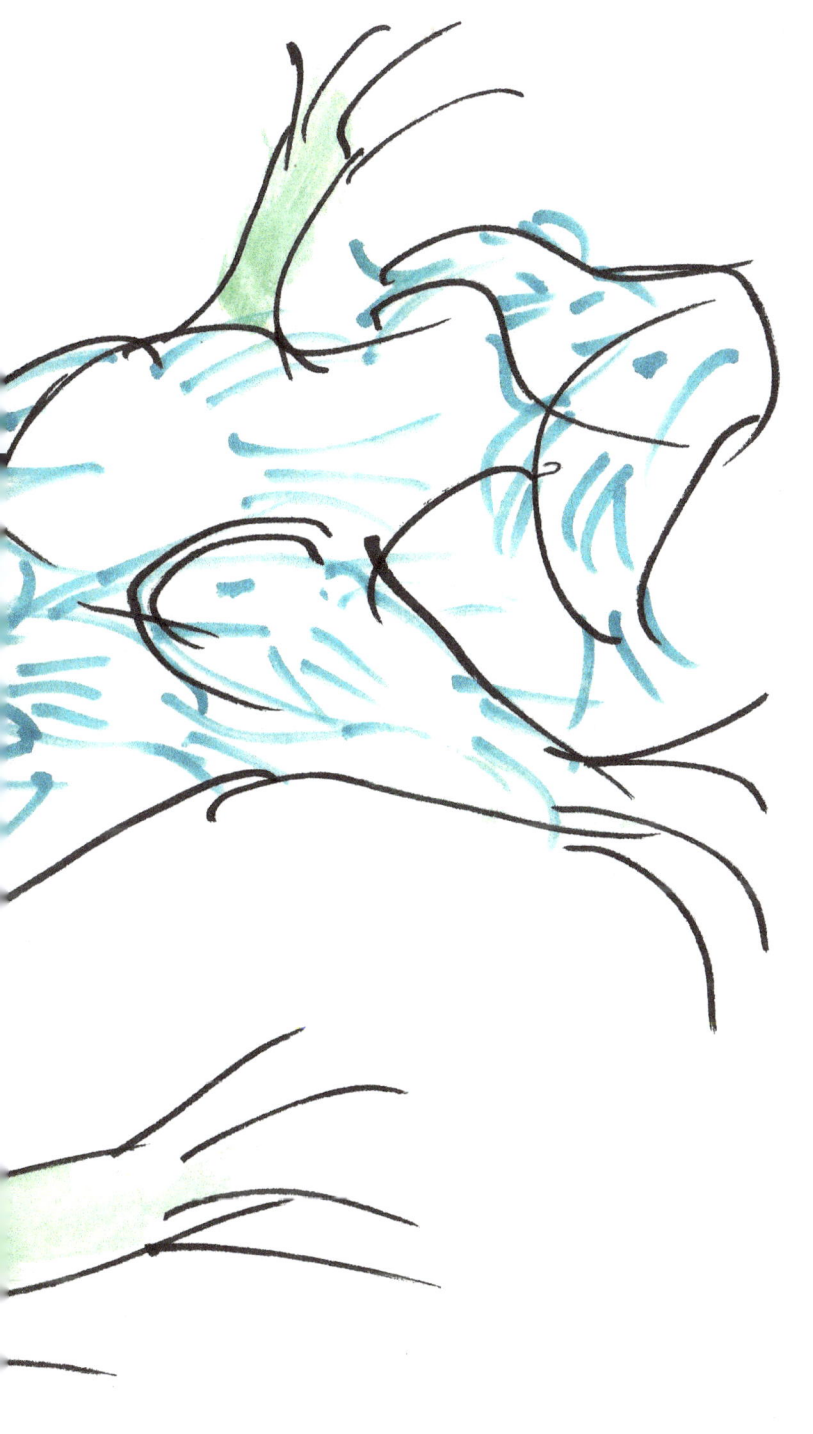

**To All the Beautyfull Weeds
That Won't Grow Straight**
For the queer youth at the Pgh Equality Center youth nights

Did they sow you on the carport concrete

Or in the crawlspace under the back porch

Water you with kerosene

Light you with a blow torch

Prune you with a cleaver

And say Grow—and then mourn

To watch your stalk

Fold in a fetal

Curve, find

The tic-tac-toe

Slashed on your leaves and

Their anxious stares returned with

Angry vacancy? How could they

Know you, fugitive bloom,

Lost in the labyrinth of your hungry roots

Seeking another soil?

Love Song (Aversion)

Did they, child, talk yet again
about the One who loves you more than
your mama and daddy, except when
you do what's unlovable
even for It (or was it them)? Did
the steely glint in those
avuncular eyes and the way
they laid their hands on
the straps that secured you,
praising that fierce idol whose
name sounded all
wrong on their tongues, tell on
the something quivering and cruel in
the cold stagnant pools of
their hearts as they put
that clamp on your balls
and turned up the juice?

AJ's Arms

say AJ loves
their autistic little bro
(the movie tatt)
& life—see that
big black ; on their wrist
among the cuts & burns right
where the veins are thickest?

ask where can AJ go &
what the fuck's one fragile kid
whose family's too
consumed with survival to know?

say love won't
save AJ, please don't
touch them, please it's
they, them, dark
silence cuts, don't
say you care then
leave, the dark
won't leave them, won't
you stay?

ask where's the soft green plot
for the fragile among
the falcons & maggots?

know AJ loves
to laugh—I heard
them, smiled, said *Until
there's nothing, there's hope*

Before You Fall

                      imagine: 2k
skyward, 30 molten stories
                          sirens smoke & uniform

frenzy below, but in your
                     crow's nest buffeted by
the cleansing blue
               the skyline

  so clear so
                    choose to fly
        beautiful, you
                          before you fall

Love Song (Separation 1)

1

Come to the window, my love—
Meat perfumes the air!
Night yawns like a gorged beast of prey
As beneath its twitching paws we sing
Fa-la-la-love is all our yesterdays
Stumbling bliss-drunk to
The dawn's fatal blow
Flesh-scummed jaws
Splintering bone

2

Frankie loved Johnny on the shithouse floor
Frankie left her heart carved in the door
Then down by the river at the stroke of night
Her dreams writhing pink on a silver barb, she
Reeled her gasping gape-mouthed tomorrows
Out of the slime

Johnny slung his jeans where the stars couldn't
 see them
Johnny swam naked through the lilies and
 leeches
A bobbing cork at the end of a pole
Johnny loved Frankie 'til no more could be said
Johnny loved Frankie 'til her pistol was red
From his bleeding hole

3

My love, let us be true
To ourselves—for love, my love, is a game
For the trenches, love sears its name
With mustard gas in our chests,
Wrenches our youth from its sockets
On bayonets and kicks us home
With pockets of muddy scrip,
Scars that we lick when it rains,
Fantasies of flight, and
Songs to sing: Fa-la-la
Yeah alright

Daughter Late (Pietas)

Just those three hours
One June afternoon, your
Greeting smile too soon
Hostage to a body in freefall, though
Your parting embrace so
Fierce, as if to pry me apart
Like the doctors did you and im-
Plant all your love for me
Next to my heart—three blinkered hours,
Backs to the abyss of the day after
And after and after. But what after
All would knowing the turn to
Come with the new sun
Have changed? Would I have
Flooded the cells of shame and fear
Where we knew each other
Those fifty years, somehow, with the light
I was learning to sing—or maybe tried

To coax out the words you'd
Stashed away, the proud-papa stuff
Girls hear on prom night? No,
You always spoke best with your eyes and arms.
It's better this way, the brute eloquence
Of that blind, unsteady hand
Reaching for mine to pull
To a mouth too weak to pucker—to suck
Like a teething infant. And now I
Find myself mourning alone for the father-
Daughter bond sprouting through
The fall's killing frosts and that
Last, absent pinch of my late-bloomed breast—
A premature harvest you plucked
To nourish you in the dark place
Where I can't follow.

Betty Grable Legs

With a note of pride
They used to say
I had Betty Grable legs
My mother, still a beauty
Half a century
Later, said one day, and I
Remembered when I
Told her, so plainly
Ill at ease, *Your*
Daughter's a looker
Remembered the sunny August
Morning five years
Before, her pained
Smile when I told her
I'm a woman—She
Has great legs
My sister added—*Thanks*
Mom, I said—remembered
The half century
Gone

Love Song (Dad)

I can't flush this love-borne malaise
desolating me like some B
noir on endless repeat: you
backlit, sprawled on the bar
sucking the old stories dry from
memory's withered teat, or guiding
your rusted out Caddy to
that old makeout spot
to chase your crimes with
the bourbon stashed in the trunk
a two bit four hour absolution
in oblivion's sloppy embrace

All the years hating
myself for all that
didn't please and all the
light I'm left, you sullen
silent ghost, is in my mirror?

Love Song (Separation 2)

When love dies, does it fossilize?
How else to explain the crushing
Ache of the silence
In those spaces you once filled?

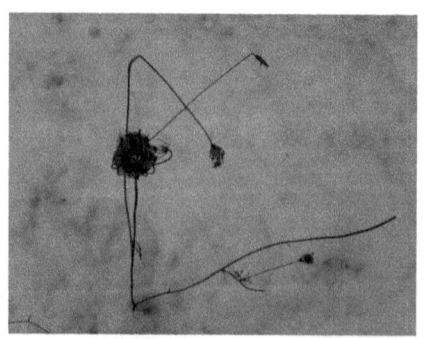

Love Song (Congruence)

How to say the wonder of
These new-found lands—the sweet
Snow-melt bubbling from this tongue,
The grace in these arms,
These hands, these fingers,
Hips and legs and feet
Of the terns' swoops, the diamond darts of
The herring shoals, the deer's tiptoe
Dances in the dawn-dewed grass or
The way the dragonflies and bees
Seem to hover in the morning sun
Out of gravity? How to convey
The marvel of gently rolling plains of fat,
The miracle of breasts?

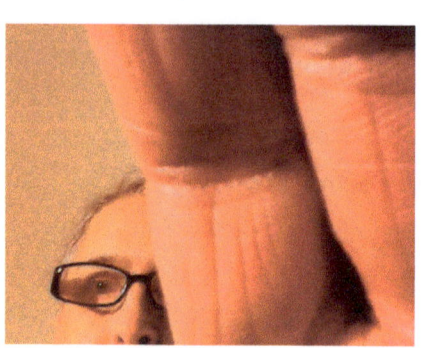

The Length of an Arm

We don't measure distance
in units like inches or
miles or light-years but
in the strain in your smile
when I mention my breasts
the half-swallowed breaths
drunk from our silences
the arc your nose traces
with the turn of your face
the length of your arm
your raised palm demarcating
intimacy's border: *just
here, and no closer*

Hope's the Drug You

Hope's the drug you
never lectured me on—hope
that I might dig through
the heaped up defenses of so
many generations and find you
bigger than you are—but then
Time with a shrug opens its door
to my foxholed decades
below the frost line watching
you laud the triumphs laid
at the tutelary altar and chalk
over the desiccated smiles, the dirt
sliding from the cracks, and the silence
of a snowbitten wood
after a winter gale
throbs through my heart. Blame's
a stupid game I won't play—

my erasure was
mine, or everyone's—and to be
known as well as loved
was a big ask, and probably
a selfish one, but when
I see it wither again
and again in the sunsoaked
nostalgia for a young world where I was
impossible, I can't help
but wonder whether
it would have been best
if you'd drowned me in the leach field
when you had the chance.

The Girl Who Vanished in Her Tomorrows

They'll tell you they couldn't see
Him now that she
Was here. Oh, the profile might recall
Him sometimes, certain things she
Said ring true, though the voice they heard
Made them somehow strange as well
As the laughter they cascaded in on, so
Like but unlike the person they knew, and
Then there were the tells they
Couldn't see, but knew others could, and
The looks she drew they'll tell you they
Didn't see, and didn't mind, and
Yet it was hard to forget
The person they no longer saw and the looks
They didn't see or mind somehow
Hinted at something precious
Threatened, and pulling
Their kids close to their sides they
Told her in soothing tones that her

Being here was an encumbrance and her
Love an inconvenience and it
Might be best if tomorrow
She wasn't here
To spare the children from
Pain they couldn't fathom, and any
Way all the world knows suffering ennobles
Others.

Cassandra

Fringe's daughter, when your lustlorn
god spat his fierce wisdom on your
virgin tongue, did you fore
see the raging herd's contempt
for a truth stammering girl—the hour's
hero rutting her while she clutched
a weeping goddess' wooden knees—
the butcher block of a vengeful queen—as you
watched the stampede to gut-garlanded slaughter?

#WalkingWhile

Walking while you, naked in the raging
Streets where you're a crime, do you sometimes
Wish for a skin of unblinking eyes,
A heart full of mustard gas, a hole
Where the fists won't find you?
Do you wish sometimes for a name
That means just you and love, a hole
Where their tongues can't touch you?

For Muhlaysia

They beat you under the Texas sun
in a goddamn parking lot, one two four
eight ten kicking punching howling
filming so they could pretend
it was everyone and not just
they who were unmanned
by a beauty that held
a mirror to their squalid smallness
a window on such a big
wonder they lost them
selves in the vertigo—
                        Girl, they
wanted you, feared you, so
bad they swarmed to snuff
out this feeling they
couldn't piss on and laugh

Remembrance (January 2013)

To 22 year old rapper Evon, suffocated with a
   plastic bag, choked with a chain, and beaten
   with wrenches and hammers in Milwaukee
   on New Year's Day
To 20 year old Nicole in Brazil, shot to
   death after the boy she kissed and his
   companheiros discovered the secret that
   shouldn't have to be a secret
To 21 year old Dannie, kidnapped and
   decapitated by an armed gang in Monterrey
To the unnamed but not nameless 22 year old
   shot in Sarasota the same day
To Ale, 24, in Buenos Aires, killed somehow the
   day after
To Fernanda, 32, of Viamo, Brazil, shot by two
   men in a car
To Tiffany of Guyana, sex worker, teenager,
   throat slit
To Nathalia, 32, stabbed in Quezon City, and
   her death mocked in the papers

To Cecilia, age not given, shot six times in
    Fortaleza
To Natalya, treinta, shot twice in Maracaibo,
    tierra del sol amada
And Jeckson and ?, killed in the same city,
And = =, killed by a car up the coast in Caracas,
    all on the 19th
To Agata, just a teen, stabbed to death in
    Camapua the day after my 49th birthday
To Romildo of Recife, stoned to death after 35
    years of life
To Alejandra, 28, neglected to death in a
    Colombian hospital after a fight
To 30 year old Indian Vinod, shot
To 36 year old Karen of Zimatlán de Álvarez,
    found stabbed and half naked
To 27 year old La Tita of Ciudad Sandino, la
    Nueva Vida, stabbed in her home by her
    date

To 18 year old Vitória of Boa Vista, stabbed to
 death by her boyfriend:
It's not all your snuffed out tomorrows
Nor the sanctioned bigotry
Nor even the ferocity
Of your murders—call them atrocities—
That sits like nine hundred pounds of lead and
 ice in my heart, but the fear
That as the motherfuckers came at you
You might for a second have felt
I deserve this.

The Girl Who Dreamed of Tornadoes

not snow squalls cuz she wasn't cold
not hurricanes, she didn't know
just why, except perhaps the way
a twister pulled you in while
ripping you apart was like
the way the voices who'd said No
Freak Faggot Monster
It all her life all
sounded like her

Night Songs

1

My love, there's blood in the water
Tonight the frenzied teeth
Flash their need and loathe all
They can't shred and swallow
The currents giddy with foam
From the slaughter, the voyeur birds'
Screams and the moon
Smiles down like a drowned child

2

What secrets, my love, not worth
The breath in the great blankness
Where your eyes swim? The tongues of
Your scars are silent, only the gone-by
Holding your hand, whispering All
You were and are

3

Memory's deadly game outs
The times you turned from fist or
Mirror, the short circuited
Moments down the rabbit's
Hole ever present or never
My love, the past is a stalker

4

Why this flinch, poised
On the edge of so
Small a moment to plunge
At his next breath, he
Or she, my love, are surely
Just words?

5

Must it be another back
Alley reckoning, your bulging black
Womb unburdened of all the
Nothing you're not, the still
Born days and weeks
And months—the forty year
Sleep that sounds, my love
A lot like death?

6

Fetal in the hollow of the razor
Tongued hours, all the papered over
Sucker punched pepper sprayed
Licked, cut, my love, the next
Minute is a conversation for the
Next minute

7

Take heed, my love, in these
Looking glass days yours
The face they fear
To see in their bathrooms
Tonight, smiling
An affirmation of all
Themselves they despise

8

My love, did she smile
Down the long nose of privilege at
The best jest Nature ever
Bred and the day
Was a clawed open wound and
The thought that she
Loosed the torrents of
Pain inside you for
Fun was your
Fondest wish?

9

Smudge out your tracks
With charcoal, wipe your palms
In your eyes, my love, your slide
Beneath the midnight
Sea's glittering ripples your
Blackest yes

10

Have you learned at last to
Surrender to sleep and
The chance your heart will
Stop before sunrise? To be wise
For you the ceasing to
Cling to life as if full
Were in lungs and another
Day you might start
Living—for what can death
Teach you, my love, who
Were born of loss?

11

My love, the world's stupid
Revenge for the good, to whom
Much, much, yet some
Times the right's just
A daisy in the mud

12

Memory's blade and the day
Teeter over tomorrow's
Maw on the tip of
A raving toddler's dooms
Daydream, my love, let's
Go watch the world burn

Love Song (Death)

At the gate that swallows sound and light
My sweetheart waits—no noir silhouette
In a backlit haze of cigarettes,
Whiskey and regret, just
A cloaked shadow, a ripple
In the black hinting at
Their curling lip, their beckoning arm,
Their embrace that's neither
Soft nor firm, warm nor cold, but true
After their fashion—no strings
Or volition, only the slow
Dumb waltz past desire's chafe
Doubt's sinkhole
Tear   breath   gravity
A last flutter in the nerves

i, scattered
After Bill's self portrait

sometimes i wander
thru peacock shimmer
raptor gardens, sometimes
float on a foaming
void under blind masks
tongue like a dead whale

sometimes i spill
out the fissures
tangled tendrils of eyes
striped, serpentine
tunnels to—yearning

sometimes i crumble, scatter
but sometimes

birds, yes, there
are birds soaring
into canyons of sky

The Girl Who Collected Feathers

wondered about the dreams of birds,
whether they yearned for the airless blue
at the roof of the sky where their cries would wither
like fresh-plucked daisies on the winter
pavement's black ice, or imaged the burrows
of the skittish things they shredded and stuffed down
their chicks' downy throats, puzzling out
safety as an embrace of snug dirt, or just
reveled in the memories of summer winds
that lifted them above the stench and the lice
to the sphere where the wrenching throbs of desire
and fear doze in a still, ceaseless fire—
call it satiety, or Paradise.

Philomela

They banged you in the dark, child
sawed off your tongue and said
cuz this is all u are but there's no
binding the eloquent hands of
a stupid freak like you
at your loom while they finger
the rough red tracks of your scarred life
laughing, those
hands filter
nothing—

What Is a Wall?

not a window's ask but
the rock-eyed gun-tongued
declaration: I do
not want to
risk bigness, know
your alien pulse
its cleansing vertigo
that's to say
Love

9:29 Is Long Enough

to dance to that old song
the way y'all used to dance
with your mom, or circle the room
with a hug for everyone, big hearted
Big Floyd, long enough
to wonder how come
this time it's you there,
under his knee, and what fantasy
he's acting, the master
of the Big House or maybe
a big cat, wishing that knee
were his teeth at your throat—
wonder what your momma would do
watching this white man
snuff out her child and stare
back like any blank-eyed predator,
any courthouse wall.

Lily Law n the Street Queens
New York City, June 1969

queenie u just know ull live 4ever
cuz u know each days ur last
summer nites in the park cuttin ur girls
bitch ain't no paint 2 cover up
all that ugly whod ur mama fuck
9 months b4 u born?
ur tongues an artists brush in a blade
cuz theres beauty in the way u
slice up all that pain tho u
scratch em with the claw of a broken bottle top
when they cut u back then
kiss n makeup cuz thats love n love
is a waltz of cats in july n cats live
9 times isnt that like
4ever? october
comes n the green world is painted
like u the yellows n reds
turn the color of shit n u
see all the shit ur tongue talks

shimmering silver under the streetlights but
decembers so cruel cuz
the bitches all want what u want n
nothing comes free from
the santas on christopher street n
maybe u see april
n maybe u dont but it dont
matter cuz queenie ur living 4ever
with 2day n the next ur last

but not 2nite
2nites a good night 2 die cuz
its hot like the airs on fire n
ur so fuckin done with Lilys shit
Lily who look at u like ur daddy used 2
Lily with her love stick wanna crack
u a cunt on the top of ur skull
n watch her cum ooze gray n red
thats the love Lily do

but not 2nite cuz
2nite Queenie is urs
2nite ur a guerilla chorus line
rubbin ur shit in Lilys popeyes n
talkin ur shit in Lilys red ears cuz
who talks sense when
2nites so fuckin hot n lilys not
ur master cuz its ur last?
turn n kick n
we r the Stonewall Grrls
when u wanna show em ur puckered pussy n say
here we r u macho fucks u wanna
piece of THIS?

The Hole

Roxsana está muerta
a los 33 años
she walked a thousand miles
cuz she feared home
more than liberty's fierce
riddle & was welcomed
as the wretched refuse
they said she was
iced in the hole
shackled, starved, surveilled
then erased
from the video
cuz her captors were jealous
of their days & nights
together gutting her for
all their garbage they dumped y por
que ella vino y dijo *Aquí*
estoy

Maenad

Agave, no tears,
Though the head you cradle
Be one you loved,
Though the blood on your tongue
Be your kin's: blessed above
All the women of Thebes,
Fueled by the god's fire,
The Bacchantes' righteous madness!

Cruel Olympus permitted
A world out of kilter,
This bountiful city
Lorded over by one who
Denied us the sun's rays,
The play of our passions,
Chained us in shadow.
Queer Dionysus,
Terrible, gentle
Savior, we hail you!

You sprang us from bondage,
Called us to revels
Under the night sky on
Sacred Cithaeron.
Hearts pregnant with fury,
Chaste but ecstatic,
Burned with your spirit:
Your cleansing white flames
Ignited the mountain!
Then came your verdict
In kind on our captor,
The man who loathed women
Transformed into woman
(His pride felled by wonder
Or something inside him)
And fed to our anger—
A terrible justice.

Queer god and goddess
Conceived in Zeus' lightning,
Through you we know all of
This world to be molten:
The very stones shimmer
With Gaia's gay lifeblood!
The fool who would dam up
Her currents will burn to
Ash in her lava.

Lady-lord of the vineyard,
Of laughter and riot,
Your imperatives rule us.
By you are imbalances
Righted, fear punished;
Monsters loosed, fences trampled.
In kind is your coming,
Liberator in friendship,
Fierce foe when rejected:
To fight you is madness
Akin to self-murder.
This fool who denied you
Now knows fools alone
Make war with volcanoes.

Agave, no tears,
Though this fool was your son:
One kiss, then draw down
Sleep's shades over eyes
Dark in death as in life
And rejoin the head
With the scraps on that table,
A jigsaw for ravens.
No tears, brave mother,
Blessed above women,
Agave, now midwife
To a rebirth of wholeness!

Indivisible
For my IFH sisters and brothers

two steps at a stride
up these crazy slopes, child
playing mountain goat

lifts the woman
tokens of hope in
hand, seeking

unborn days in the
indian summer
shimmer:

air-parched, sole-sore
her skin smelling
like sunlight

The Girl Who Loves Marilyn Monroe
For Melissa

She loves Marilyn Monroe and good liquor
And carries a pistol in her purse
She has the hands of a carpenter
A southern senator's baritone
And dreams of breasts big as grapefruits

As the late day sun glows through
The kitchen curtains, she'll tell you
Of the shelves she's put in
And her silver bobbed wig
And her journey to New Hope
Where she spoke of her purse strings and
    eyebrows and balls
And watched a blonde doctor fondle her pecs
The size of grapefruits will be best
And the soft late day sun lights up her talk
And the framed prints of
Marilyn Monroe hung
Floor to ceiling
In the next room
The levity comes and goes

She feels the suck of time's sinkhole
On her sagging frame
And the ache of needs
She doesn't want, and can't explain
And the stings of a swarm disinclined
To seek out beauty in forms
Its pundits don't prescribe
Her hangdog eyes press us: *This*
And no more?
Her smile is an achievement

Except when she speaks of the tenderness
In her budding chest—the tangerines
That are her glimpse of
The girl she might have been—
And the comfort of friends
And Marilyn Monroe
The platinum sun
In her Norma Jeane sky

The Girls Who Saw the Dinosaur Bones
For Crystalynn (1954–2020)

The morning her penny dropped, she says, was
A selfie at the end of a half-century nod
And so (she says) she threw out her pants
Stopped drinking and smoking herself to death
And found she liked being fucked by men
And driving cross-country, alive to the Rockies'
Rugged majesty and the pain
From some neuromuscular thing that's
Withering her legs and won't let her stay
On her feet for long—*What else to do?*
She'll laugh as she wrings
Her grimace to a grin
With each step cuz there's so much
Living to squeeze into so
Little life. But when
She saw the dinosaur bones
It's like a part of her was home: there
They were, the butts of a cosmic joke—

Like us, she says—the world they ruled
Flooded with dust from a chance meetup with
A space rock, and an eon's eyeblink
After they were gone; now
Squealing children darted beneath
Their colossal useless limbs that,
Bored to brown stone by the 200 million
Years' indifference, hung
Welded together with iron rods
In a tableau of wrath, the stick-figure gods
From a dream no bender can ever
Smudge out. *What else to do*
But laugh? At which
My eye was drawn to the campiest beast
In the whole oneiric bestiary,
Little Caudipteryx, fierce in the shadow
Of the Tyrant King, a feathered and clawed
Dancing lizard in bird drag—but no!

Evolution didn't play even
The mashups for laughs: obeying its nature
Like all of us do, it strove to
Realize the beauty it knew,
And if as for so many of us
Its materials were not
What others had got—
Well so what? And I smiled
To this long silenced sweet
Terrible call echoing through
My absurdity—*What else to do
After all?*

Dancing with Nicky

pulling pulling me, me, those eyes
pulling me into your orbit, spirals
tighter as your eyelids slide
into their sleepy embrace and
dropping through my
own fierce air burns
up the freak, a hole in
the clouds, dizzy green
worlds, lips
touch, part
waltzing butterflies

Love Song (Mom)

So many times unkind
assumptions
leaching from my fault lines

have muddied our moments
together, and yet here
you are now, again, with

your beautiful courage
after so many
scarring years, telling me

how beautiful I am and that
you love me, and some-
how, again, the salve

I crave shocks, and I
cower in shadow's
familial embrace from

the sweet lesson
of surrender

Love Song ( )

My love, my heart's a balled fist:
Unclench it with your tender patience.
Please don't run when I cough up
The half century's toxins I've swallowed.
Don't mind overmuch when I cut
Myself, or fall in a hole
Cursing what I've been, what I am, know
The thought of your disdain
Terrifies me. Please
Don't shrink if you should spring
An untamed thing in me—
Don't shudder at its needs
Or stop when I scream
Or laugh when I ask you

Not to touch me there. Please
Don't see what greets me
In my mirror when I rise, look
Through this skin I'm sloughing
Like a child spying the ocean's jewels
At the bottom of a tidal pool. My love,
Hold me tight under the June night sky,
Pull me into your half moon,
Push your lips through mine and
Speak in my innermost place
The sweetest secret you know.

After and Before (Four Photos)

The "before" and "after" photos are one of the most trite tropes about the lives of trans folks, and one of the most distorting. *First man, now woman* (or vice versa) homogenizes our idiosyncratic journeys, and reduces our quest for congruence to an extreme makeover, a skin-deep process undertaken for reasons that are inscrutable, bizarre, and probably perverse.

◘

Mirror, mirror
life in splinters
\♀\
\\⚧\\
\\\♂\\\
\\\\I\\\\

◘

4

It's my first selfie, or at least the first one I was happy with. I'm in the old steel city of Johnstown, PA, standing near the terminus of the inclined plane trolley at the summit of one of the ridges rimming the valley where the city sits. My face, neck, and the tops of my shoulders occupy the left half of the frame. The leafy branches of a tree soften the upper right corner. Both are in shadow with the exception of the tip of one of the tree's branches. In the background, there's a block of pale blue cloudless sky, and beneath it, the valley's opposite ridge. The ridge is awash in sunshine, and deep veins crisscross its forested slopes at different angles where the trees have been clear cut for roads or utility lines, suggesting a green arroyo bearing the scars of the recent seasonal runoff.

One reason I like this image is that I find its compositional elements appealing. The contrasts between foreground shadow and luminous background, between the verticality of my face and the mostly invisible tree, and the supine ridge. The way my gaze, directed to the right (my left) and slightly down, follows the gentle slope of the ridge behind me. More than these, though, I'm happy that I managed to capture an expression that isn't self-conscious or defensive. My eyes are pensive, resolved, a little sad. My lips are at rest, as if unaware of the camera.

The friend I'm visiting has chided me frequently for not smiling for pictures. I've often wished I could summon the effortless radiance that is one of my sister's special gifts. But the truth is that I've long mistrusted cameras, just as I've avoided mirrors, fearing what they would show me.

It's the Fourth of July weekend, 2014, almost three months after I appeared in the Allegheny County Court of Common Pleas to petition to have my legal name changed. The proceeding took perhaps five minutes. It was the culmination of a nearly three-month process that began the day after my 50th birthday in late January, a similarly sunny though frigid day, in a conference room of a large law firm in a downtown Pittsburgh skyscraper. I'd signed up shortly before then with a corporate initiative called the Name Change Project, which was providing *pro bono* legal assistance to trans folks like me, and my case had been assigned to two young attorneys, both women. They stood on either side of me during my April 10 court date, and the judge, an old Irishman named O'Reilly, devoted half the hearing to chastising them for cheating on their service requirement. "A name change petition is like filling out a driver's license form!"

That day in April was also warm and sunny. I marked this self-affirming step by wearing a new pair of pumps, and since I had to do a fair bit of walking to and in the court building, my feet were blistering in a few spots by the time I left. My old friend Sue when I mentioned this afterwards admonished me: "NEVER EVER EVER go ANYwhere in new shoes." She also told me she'd "cracked herself up" a few days before when she reflected on the differences between our recent birthdays (we were born on the same day). "I challenged myself to sing at my party, and I was so frightened!"

We met when we were 20 at the University of Edinburgh in Scotland, where we spent our junior year of college. That year, I tried for the first time to talk to other people about my struggles with my gender identity.

The day after my 50th birthday, I drove from the downtown meeting to a Staples in a neighborhood near where I live to photocopy and mail a four-page coming out letter to my old friends. Sue called early the following week, and we talked for a couple of hours. She told me at the start of the conversation that she'd waited a day after receiving the letter to reach out because she wanted to begin working through the "thousands of conflicting feelings" she had about it with her counselor first. She admitted late in the call that one of the strongest of those feelings was the fear that all the years of our friendship were lost.

During the July Fourth weekend, one of my friend's paramours was also visiting her. He'd driven from Ohio on his motorcycle. I remember sitting on her porch with him talking about guns. He always carried one with him, he said. He retrieved it at one point and handed it to me, and I held it as if it were a sleeping rattlesnake, even though he assured me the safety was on. I'd shot a gun only once, in my twenties during my first marriage.

I learned later from my friend that her paramour found me attractive. This news was both flattering and unsettling. I wasn't attracted to men—I'd had only one encounter, in Edinburgh, which I'd enjoyed but hadn't been aroused by—but more to the point, I was struggling to imagine how anyone could be turned on by my hybrid body. What did it mean to be a lesbian with a penis? My friend had found she loved sex with men, and had had several weekend assignations and a couple of longer-term relationships. Before transitioning, she was married for many years and had two grown children; I was childless after two marriages. I told her more than once that I envied her sexual freedom.

Past and future shimmer in this photo. I'm resting in the shade after a six-month flurry of activity, and the four-plus decades of trauma that preceded them. I've momentarily turned my back on the sun-soaked expanse of the months and years ahead. Pensive, resolved, a little sad. I will often return to the shadows, not always by choice, going forward.

◘

Self-knowledge, the process of growing from a retrospective into a proactive being, isn't a straightforward thing, of course. Its relationship with expectation is particularly complex. Those of us who see mostly what we're told we should see when we look inside, tend to grow into ourselves more easily but less consciously. Those of us who see things we're told we shouldn't see tend to become self-aware earlier—since self is in its most rudimentary sense the awareness of being distinct from—but to struggle to embrace what we see. Self-knowledge requires both awareness and acceptance. Lacking the former, we wallow in privilege and prejudice. Without the latter, we wither or bleed out.

◘

Laughter dissolves boundaries. I was afraid to laugh.

     Joy Ladin, *Through the Door of Life*

◘

2

During my spring break at the University of Edinburgh, I traveled by train to Greece with two of my flatmates, Hilary and Chris, and a quirky, reclusive friend of Chris's also named Chris. Hilary took this photo. We're on the island of Paros for the day, I think, waiting for a ferry to take us to Santorini.

  She's been trying for a couple of days to get me to laugh, or at least smile, without reservation, and this is one of the most unguarded moments I remember from the trip (at least when I wasn't drinking). Still, what strikes me most about the image is my hesitancy to trust her. My smile is pinched at the corners, my eyes almost closed, my head tossed back as if trying to get as far away from the camera as my neck will allow. I could be turning towards her, but I know I want to run, and my half profile is an act of will.

We'll grow closer over the course of the trip, though I'll separate from her and the others on the way back to Scotland to spend a day in Luxembourg. My initial plan is to go to Denmark, but I decide I don't have enough time. Denmark's appeal has to do with the romance I attached to Scandinavia as a sort of spirit animal for my home state of Maine enriched by an Old World heritage. It will be two decades before I learn about American trans pioneer Christine Jorgensen's journey there in the early 1950s to start hormone replacement therapy and undergo a series of gender affirming surgeries, and 30 years before I hear of "Danish girl" Lili Elbe.

Shortly after the start of our final term, I begin sleeping in Hilary's room. We make out sometimes, and try to have sex, but I'm afraid, and can't get hard. I'm humiliated, but she's patient. I try to tell her about my gender struggles, but I seize up whenever I think about them, unable to see them as other than monstrous. I'll have a similar experience in my late 40s when I come out to my parents, though instead of slumping into numbed silence, I'll weep for several seconds before forcing the first words out of my mouth.

My flatmate Chris, I discovered soon after we met the previous fall, had as a boy summered every year with his family on an island near where I grew up. Both of his parents were academics. We had an easy friendship. Hilary, by contrast, exploded into my life. Her passion and raw vulnerability, so foreign to my yankee upbringing, modeled a terrifying, exhilarating liberation that quickly came to seem like a life and death choice. They also stood in stark contrast to the frosty reserve of the Scots, and she was soon declaring how unhappy she was there, and that she would be leaving at the end of the fall term rather than staying for the whole year. The prospect filled me with dread.

Midway through my sophomore year at Haverford College, I experienced a spiritual crisis that had been mounting through my teens. I hated the way puberty hijacked my slender, androgynous body, and loathed myself for hating it and not embracing being male, and by the time I turned 20, I couldn't repress this conflict any longer. That winter I passed in a near lightless hole.

Two episodes from those weeks stand out. In the first, I'm lying on my bed in the dark late one afternoon, and all at once I feel myself rise into a sitting position halfway out of my body. I see a gray shade emerge out of a swirling fog of figures that I recognize as one of my uncles (still alive at the time). "Let's go fishing," he says. With a jolt, I plunge back into my body.

A few weeks later, around the start of spring, I'm sitting on my dorm room floor one night with my lamp on listening to a record by an old acid rock band from Texas called the 13th Floor Elevators. One of my suite mates lived in New York City, and I'd arranged for him to pick it up in a Greenwich Village shop for me over the Christmas break. The record was already growing familiar, but for whatever reason, this time its first song's urging to "slip inside this house as you pass by" cracks open a door inside me and floods me with light, and so much that had seemed impossibly remote is in an instant there at hand. I can choose to walk with others instead of alone—to walk in daylight instead of darkness—to live instead of die. I tear up and say to myself over and over, "I'm saved!"

A Saturday morning in February three decades later, I weep convulsively for a half hour when for the first time I access the repressed pain inside me, embrace the girl I've been denying since childhood. Whisper repeatedly, "Please forgive me."

Hilary and I lived together in San Antonio

(where she went to college) that summer and the next, moved to Philadelphia (near my college) for a couple of years, moved to Alabama (where she was from) and got married, and divorced a decade later.

I'm holding myself in a half profile, but I so want to run towards her, smiling, laughing freely. The goatee and the yellow scarf puffing out of my old khaki windbreaker mark my budding transition from drab smalltown New Englander to something more flamboyantly bohemian and (on the DL) gender variant. But I'm squinting in fear of the changes blooming in the blaze of this Mediterranean spring day.

◘

When I look at photos of myself from even just ten years ago, I struggle to occupy the scene in my mind. I likely recognize the setting, and may remember the occasion when the photo was taken, but it's hard to recall what it felt like being me in that moment, interacting with that setting and the other people in it. This isn't unusual in kind—the passing of time robs everyone of the immediacy of all but the most formative moments—but rather in degree. The look in the eyes of that melancholy being I recognize as myself often strikes me as almost alien, and any account I give of her in such instances is in no small measure speculative.

◘

Prince: The Beast is no more. It was I, Beauty. My parents wouldn't believe in fairy tales. The fairies punished them through me. I could only be saved by a look of love.

Beauty: Are such miracles possible?
Jean Cocteau, *La belle et la bête*

◘

3

In 2008, Pascale and I went on what was to be our last vacation together, to Grand Turk Island. We would separate a year later, and divorce the summer after that. Grand Turk is part of the Turks and Caicos, a small cluster of islands due north of Haiti, where her family was from. A couple of years earlier, we spent several days in Jamaica, and we traveled to Mexico together for a week shortly before we were married in the spring of 2003, and honeymooned in Brazil. We never visited Haiti.

I needed to renew my passport for that last trip, and when a few years ago I retrieved it from my files to submit with my application to change my name and gender, my old photo took me aback. My mouth's downward droop made my face look doughy. My hair was short and thinning on top. But it was my leaden expression that arrested my attention. I was staring off to my left, at the horizon or the space right before me, into my future or past or present. Or not.

We met at a mutual friend's wedding near Ann Arbor, Michigan, in the fall of 1997. I hoped this time would be different. Hilary and I had been bound by a strong sense of kinship and mutual concern, but Pascale and I were "in love," in my case at first sight. Could love do what friendship hadn't and cure me of my gender struggles? I decided not to tell her about this part of me, fearing it would poison the well before that love had a chance to work its wished for magic.

At our wedding, my dad was my best man. A farm kid and smalltown lawyer, he was out of his depth in our multicultural New York milieu. I asked him because he'd embraced her, and because I loved him, but also because I wanted to get it right this time.

I left Austin, where I was an ABD English grad student, to move in with Pascale at the end of 1999. I hoped this time would be different. I'd grown a beard that fall. We made love a lot for the next year or two. We lived in a one bedroom sublet in Alphabet City, then in the Bronx when another sublet in Brooklyn fell through the day of our move, then in Queens, then we bought a small house the fall after we were married and settled in suburban New Jersey. She had a blue chip law degree, but bounced from the Brooklyn DA's office to private practice to academic advisory positions at two area law schools, while I was unable to secure a tenure track teaching position, and shuffled from one one-year appointment to the next.

When Hilary and I moved to Alabama so she could attend law school, I embraced the role of provider, though with just a B.A. in English I made under $20,000 working at an ad agency and then as a technical writer at a large bank during her first year. Trying to get it right.

The second time Pascale and I saw each other was the summer after we met. She had just returned to the States from South Africa. I was visiting my sister in Boston, and she took the train from New York, where she was staying with her mom, to join us for a day. That night the two of us lay on the sofa bed in my sis's living room for hours talking. At one point, she went to the kitchen to get a glass of water, and I made a decision. When she returned and lay down facing me, I said I had something to tell her, and asked her to scoot closer. She did. I asked her to scoot closer still. She did, and I closed my eyes and rested my lips on hers for a second or two. When I opened my eyes again, hers were big and glowing in gentle, deep disorientation. She rolled over and pressed her body into mine, and I wrapped my arms around her, making no attempt to hide my arousal. We lay there without speaking until she began to doze.

Our wedding and reception were held at the Riverside Church in Harlem on a cool, overcast day in March. That morning, I took the subway downtown to get my hair cut. I didn't share with the barber, an older Nuyorican man I'd been going to almost since I moved to the city, what was looming.

Straight A's, top-tier private college, marriage, grad school, "doctor," marriage—trying, always, to get it right. I told my folks my marriage was failing when I spent Christmas with them at the end of 2007. Pascale hadn't come up with me.

Our time in Grand Turk was cordial but strained. When we weren't snorkeling or eating, she sunbathed in front of our seaside cottage while I explored the island. Before we flew down, my mom expressed her hope that this trip would rekindle our relationship. The person in the passport photo knows that won't happen.

The following year, Pascale and I will sell our house and separate. The person in the passport photo knows that will happen. The economy will nosedive into a global recession, my current teaching appointment won't be renewed, I'll apply for unemployment and move back in with my parents at the start of October, and my dad will almost die from a heart attack six weeks later. The person in the passport photo knows none of this, and she has only begun to admit to herself why she's wearing that expression. The photo's blank background is emblematic.

I had conversations with myself through my teens and early 20s, and periodically after that, about suicide: no matter how bad things got, I told myself, I wouldn't die. But suicides don't always require pills, rope, or razors. When I talked with my sister a few years ago about seeing my old passport photo, I started crying. The person gazing at, or rather past me, I said, was so obviously miserable. "Flatlined" would have been more apt.

◘

Not long ago, I recognized that my spotty memory even for recent events has to do with a coping mechanism I developed when I was very young. This mechanism was a function of the trauma I experienced when I became aware that who I knew myself to be was for some reason deeply bad and wrong. It took the form of recoiling from the present moment to shield myself—the person I knew myself to be—from whatever danger might lurk there. Over time, what I first did out of fear became reflexive, and to this day, I have to make a conscious effort to be present, and to commit to memory the things I know I'll want later.

◘

A work buddy and I had an exchange a while back about our respective struggles when we were young, and I told her I was too stubborn to die. Sometimes survival is the greatest expression of hope.

◘

1

I don't remember much from my childhood. It wasn't to outward appearances an unhappy one. I had friends. I did well in school. I played basketball and Little League, and later soccer. I was in the school plays in high school, and had some major roles. In grade school, I picked up the clarinet, the same instrument my best friend Joe chose, the same instrument my mom played when she was a girl (my brother, a year younger than me, opted for the trumpet). Summers I spent on the beach in front of our house, romping through the nearby woods, or sailing with my family. I always had passions: toy cars when I was two, dinosaurs and maps soon after, tropical fish and stamp collecting in grade school, in high school record collecting. But casting its shadow over everything from before I can remember was my awareness of being other—a freak.

One Friday night early in 2018 at a weekly hangout night for queer youth that for a time I co-facilitated, several of us, volunteers and kids, sat around a long table playing Big Talk, a get-acquainted game in which participants answer questions about themselves on cards drawn at random. One card asked: "What time in your life would you like to go back to, and why?" We went around the table, and when my turn came, I said I wanted to return to when I was three because I wanted to ask my young self who she knew herself to be?

For a time I thought secrets fundamental to who I was were submerged in my repressed memories of early childhood, faint and fragmentary like short wave radio signals bobbing in and out of the trauma and distance. Accessing them, I imagined, would fill in my blanks, make me more whole.

What would she say if I asked her if she knows she's a girl, or if she wants to be a girl? Would she have the words to tell me? Would she trust me enough?

For a time I imagined a submerged life that the girl inside me had led all those years a male persona occupied her place—posited this life as my real one.

The child in this grainy black and white image looks to her left past the picture taker, as if she's already learning to distrust cameras. She's leaning forward like she's poised to leap somewhere, her hands resting on the tops of her thighs—or is she pushing herself down? Her right hand reaches for the cracker pinched between the thumb and middle finger of her left. The index finger of her left hand points down, or perhaps at the space between her legs, as if to say, *To be fed, clothed, sheltered–loved–I have to accept what they say I am.* When I was a little older, I would sit on the toilet pinching that little nob of flesh between my thighs and gazing at the smooth triangle that remained, hardly daring to wish. My father scolded me for peeing sitting down.

Would she recognize how our mom and dad, our grandparents, our aunts and uncles and cousins, our neighbors, our playmates were telling her out of earnest, loving fear they had no way of fathoming to hate who she was?

I want to hold her in my arms and tell her not to be afraid. I want to tell her she's not alone, tell her other people love her more than she knows, tell her things will get better than she can imagine. I want to tell her how beautiful she is.

Notes on the Poems

"Before You Fall" (p. 26): The morning the planes struck the World Trade Center towers, I was teaching a class on Gothic fiction at Queens College, CUNY. I remember the clear view of the Manhattan skyline we had from the western end of the campus, and I remember too hearing reports and seeing images sometime after of people who'd been stranded in the upper floors of the towers leaping to their deaths, some of them holding hands, shortly before the buildings collapsed. I married for the second time 18 months later.

"For Muhlaysia" (p. 49): The attack on 23-year-old Muhlaysia Booker described here took place in Dallas on April 12, 2019. Muhlaysia sustained a concussion and a fractured wrist from it. A video of the incident went viral on social media, and drew national attention to her case. A month later, on the morning of May 18, an official from the Dallas P.D. announced that she had been found "lying facedown in the street," shot to death. Her primary April assailant had been released from police custody by this point, and was not linked to the murder. He was charged with felony aggravated assault, but later convicted of the lesser charge of misdemeanor assault. Another man was arrested on June 5, and charged with Muhlaysia's murder and the murders of two other people, neither of them trans. The great majority of the 20+ confirmed murders of trans/gender diverse folks in 2019 were of trans women of color, a trend that has continued the past couple of years. The ongoing plight of my sisters is a five-alarm human rights issue.

"Remembrance (January 2013)" (p. 51): This piece draws on the list of murder victims compiled annually for the Transgender Day of Remembrance (TDOR) observed across the U.S. and Canada, and in cities around the globe, in mid-November. I started hormone replacement therapy in March 2013.

"i, scattered" (p. 71): My brother Bill was diagnosed with Parkinson's in spring 2019. Since then, he has done a series of intricate pencil drawings like this one, entitled *Synapse*, which he describes as "a self portrait based upon my journey through" the disease.

"The Hole" (p. 85): Roxsana Hernández came to the U.S. in the spring of 2018 from Honduras as part of a migrant "caravan." She was detained by Immigration and Customs Enforcement (I.C.E.) in early May, and died a couple of weeks later of dehydration and H.I.V.-related complications. According to advocacy group the Transgender Law Center, an independent autopsy of Roxsana they co-sponsored with the law office representing her family in a wrongful death suit found that "she had deep bruising and injuries consistent with physical abuse with a baton or asp while she was handcuffed" in custody. It was later discovered that the surveillance video of her time in an I.C.E.-contracted New Mexico prison shortly before she died had been deleted. An official at the prison said that video was retained for only around 90 days due to limited storage capacity—this despite the legal proceedings already underway on Roxsana's behalf (the autopsy was performed on June 8).

Acknowledgements

The following poems have appeared previously (many have been revised for inclusion here):

AJ's Arms, Dancing with Nicky, Love Song (Aversion), Love Song (Dad), The Girl with Eyes of the Sea, The Hole, "You Have Two Sons" [*BlazeVOX20* (Spring 2020)]

i, scattered [*Ekphrastic Review* (June 22, 2021)]

The Length of an Arm [*Lavender Review* 19 (June 2019)]

9:29 Is Long Enough [*Medium.com* (June 8, 2020)]

The Girl Who Loves Marilyn Monroe [*Outrider Review* 2.3 (2015)]

Medusa, Philomela [*Scrivener Creative Review* 44 (April 2019)]

Remembrance (January 2013) [*S/tick 2.4: OUTreach* (Summer 2015)]

Lily Law n the Street Queens, To All the Beautyfull Weeds That Won't Grow Straight [*S/tick 13.2: Repeat Defenders* (Winter 2018)]

For Muhlaysia, Night Songs (sections 1-6, 8) [*S/tick 4.3: Feminists on Guard* (Fall 2019)]

A big thanks to Sarah-Jean Krahn and Katherine Davis at don't die press for their support and encouragement over the past few years.

About the Author

A Maine native but an academic gypsy for much of her adult life, Anastasia Walker is a poet, essayist, and scholar who now calls the Pittsburgh area home. Poems of hers have appeared in several journals. Two of her autobiographical essays came out in the spring of 2020: "Memory's Disavowed Daughter" (*Fourth Genre* 22:1) and "Selling My Record Collection" (*Shenandoah* 69:2). Through 2016-17, she blogged for *Huffington Post* on trans and LGBTQ+ issues, and since spring 2019 she has posted occasional pieces on politics, social media, and LGBTQ+ issues on *Medium*. She also has a YouTube channel where she posts low-tech music videos of obscure records she owns (or used to). Please visit her blog, *The Girl Who Wasn't and Is*, for information on all this and more: https://anastasiaswalker.blogspot.com/.

Anastasia volunteers for the Transgender Law Center's Prison Mail program, and is a proud member of her community's Indivisible group. She's a passionate amateur photographer and musicologist, and loves going for long walks and (when she visits home in the summers) swimming in the ocean.

Also published by bd-studios.com

Poetry Books

Georgia Dusk by Dudgrick Bevins & luke kurtis

Route 4, Box 358 by Dudgrick Bevins

Train to Providence by William Doreski & Rodger Kingston

Angkor Wat by luke kurtis

exam(i)nation by luke kurtis

the immeasurable fold by luke kurtis

(This Is Not A) Mixtape for the End of the World by Daniel M. Shapiro

Artists' Books

The Animal Book by Michael Harren

Tentative Armor by Michael Harren

Springtime in Byzantium by luke kurtis

Here Nor There by Sam Rosenthal

Just One More by Jonathan David Smyth

Architecture and Mortality by Donald Tarantino

The Male Nude by Michael Tice

Retrospective by Michael Tice

www.ingramcontent.com/pod-product-compliance
Lightning Source LLC
Chambersburg PA
CBHW041129110526
44592CB00020B/2735